My Neighborhood
The Hospital
Aaron Carr

EMERGENCY

Clearance 9'-0"

Clearance 9'-0"

EMERGENCY ROOM
PATIENT WALK-IN ENTRANCE

PARAMEDICS

AV² provides enriched content that supplements and complements this book. Weigl's AV² books strive to create inspired learning and engage young minds in a total learning experience.

Your AV² Media Enhanced books come alive with...

Audio
Listen to sections of the book read aloud.

Video
Watch informative video clips.

Embedded Weblinks
Gain additional information for research.

Try This!
Complete activities and hands-on experiments.

Key Words
Study vocabulary, and complete a matching word activity.

Quizzes
Test your knowledge.

Slide Show
View images and captions, and prepare a presentation.

... and much, much more!

Go to www.av2books.com, and enter this book's unique code.

BOOK CODE

V342130

AV² by Weigl brings you media enhanced books that support active learning.

Published by AV² by Weigl
350 5th Avenue, 59th Floor New York, NY 10118
Website: www.av2books.com   www.weigl.com

Library of Congress Cataloging-in-Publication Data

Carr, Aaron.
 The hospital / Aaron Carr.
   pages cm. -- (My neighborhood)
Audience: K to grade 3.
 ISBN 978-1-62127-345-5 (hardcover : alk. paper) -- ISBN 978-1-62127-350-9 (softcover : alk. paper)
 1. Hospitals--Juvenile literature. 2. Fire fighters--Juvenile literature. 3. Young volunteers in community development--Juvenile literature. 4. Civic improvement--Juvenile literature. I. Title.
 RA963.5.C35 2014
 362.11--dc23
                              2013006832

Printed in the United States of America in North Mankato, Minnesota
1 2 3 4 5 6 7 8 9 0   17 16 15 14 13

032013
WEP300113

Project Coordinator: Megan Cuthbert and Heather Kissock Design: Mandy Christiansen

Weigl acknowledges Getty Images as the primary image supplier for this title.

The Hospital

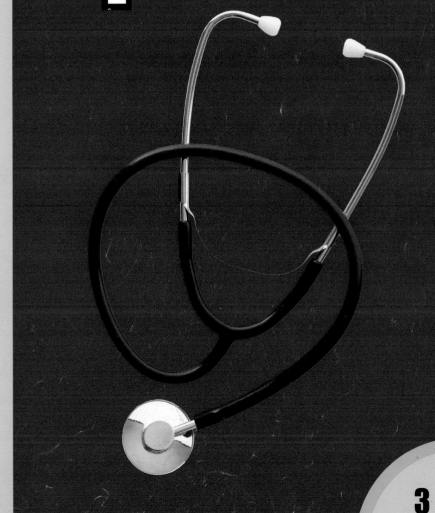

CONTENTS

This is my neighborhood.

The hospital is in my neighborhood.

My family and I go to the hospital when we are not feeling well.

The hospital has machines
that show if we are sick.

Doctors check on me
when I am in the hospital.

They see if I am well enough to go home.

9

Nurses help me when I am sick.

They help the doctors take care of me.

11

Doctors and nurses use tools to help me and my family.

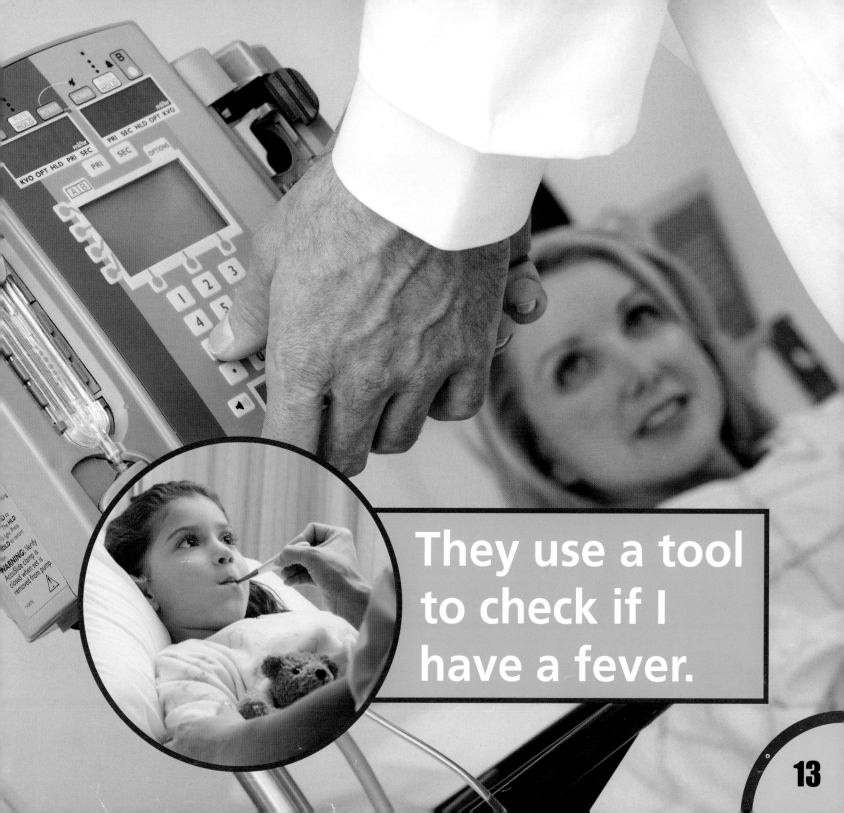

They use a tool to check if I have a fever.

13

People from my neighborhood help in the hospital.

They bring gifts and talk with people who are sick.

Sometimes the hospital has classes.

These classes teach the people in my neighborhood how to help others.

I can visit the hospital with my class from school.

18

My friends and I can ask the doctors and nurses questions about the hospital.

I often see doctors and nurses in my neighborhood.

They check to make sure people get better.

See what you have learned about hospitals.

Which of these pictures does not show a hospital?

KEY WORDS

Research has shown that as much as 65 percent of all written material published in English is made up of 300 words. These 300 words cannot be taught using pictures or learned by sounding them out. They must be recognized by sight. This book contains 47 common sight words to help young readers improve their reading fluency and comprehension. This book also teaches young readers several important content words, such as proper nouns. These words are paired with pictures to aid in learning and improve understanding.

Page	Sight Words First Appearance
4	is, my, this
5	in, the
6	and, are, family, go, I, not, to, we, well, when
7	has, if, show, that
8	am, me, on
9	enough, home, see, they
10	help
11	of, take
12	use
13	a, have
14	from, people
15	talk, who, with
16	sometimes
17	how, others, these
18	can, school
19	about
20	often
21	get, make

Page	Content Words First Appearance
4	neighborhood
5	hospital
7	machines
8	doctors
10	nurses
12	tools
13	fever
15	gifts
16	classes
19	friends, questions

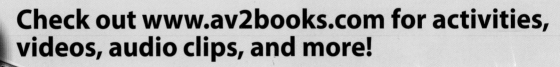